The Secret Life of The
NEW FOREST

Eric Ashby

The Secret Life of The NEW FOREST

Eric Ashby

Introduction by Richard Mabey

Chatto & Windus
LONDON

Published in 1989 by
Chatto & Windus Limited
30 Bedford Square
London WC1B 3SG

A CIP catalogue record for this book is available from the
British Library.

ISBN 0 7011 3404 6

Photoset by Rowland Phototypesetting Limited
Bury St Edmunds, Suffolk

Printed in Great Britain by
Butler & Tanner Limited
Frome, Somerset

❧ CONTENTS ☙

INTRODUCTION

Like millions of other viewers, I first became aware of Eric Ashby on a January night in 1961, when his spellbinding debut film *The Unknown Forest* was shown on BBC television, and in 45 minutes permanently changed the standards for home-grown wildlife documentaries. Anyone brought up on modern natural history films may find it hard to appreciate the impact made by this intimate look into the lives of our native animals. For much of the 1950s wildlife documentary had been dominated by globetrotting naturalists like Armand and Michaela Denis and Hans and Lotte Hass. Their films were fast-moving, exotic, superbly photographed, but presented a picture of nature as something impossibly remote and romantic – and the animals themselves, on occasions, as little more than free-range circus performers.

By the side of these, Eric Ashby's quiet, respectful cameos of foxes and badgers were a revelation. They had an austere dignity and a vivid sense of place. Many of the details of the film have faded from my memory, but I have a sharp recollection of its mood – of its contrast of early morning light and dappled shade, of animals held simply but enthrallingly in the centre of the frame, of an amiably decrepit backcloth that could only have been an ancient English wood; and, at a more personal level, of the transformation of the image of a place that I had visited since I was a boy.

It was difficult, that year, to consider Eric's work separately from the revolutions that were happening in other areas of documentary in cinema and radio, and their common move towards the celebration of local culture and ordinary experience. The film-maker himself also seemed to belong to the new mood. Ashby was unassuming to a fault, committed to working in the place where he lived, and showed no taste for the glamorous life of the professional film-maker. Not long after *The Unknown Forest* was first screened he was christened 'the silent watcher'; and a glimpse of his shadowy figure crouched by a tree, yards from an intrigued fox or deer (a little Hitchcockian indulgence in several of his films) was about all the public ever saw of him. Few people realised then what a body of hard work and hard-won wisdom lay behind his unobtrusive, almost donnish exterior. Eric had been making nature films since 1935 when he was only seventeen, and had taken his first still photograph – a terrier nosing at a hedgehog – five years before that. Even in those early days he was under the spell of the New Forest, and in 1953 put down permanent roots in a cottage on its western edge. Since then he has built up an incomparable photographic record of its creatures, landscapes, seasonal moods and moments of sadness. He has become recognised as the champion of the Forest wildlife, and his pictures are not so much detached scientific records as portraits – the animals' best shots.

This book is a selection of half a century of Eric Ashby's New Forest photographs. Even from the quickest glance it will be clear that they share many of the qualities of his films. There is a winning modesty about them, a sense that the subject is more important than the photographer and his stylistic niceties. They are packed with insights and with the condensed understanding that comes from long and patient contemplation of that mysterious other existence of animals.

Yet what shines through is not nature's 'otherness' at all, but its generosity and lack of malice, the harmony that ultimately transcends its sometimes disturbing and violent surface details. It is no insult to Eric's technical skill to say that the collection is, in many senses, a family album as well as a naturalist's portfolio. The pictures – even the most light-hearted ones – tug at many

Above One of Eric Ashby's earliest photographs, 20 June 1931.

Right 1933, using the same camera as for the fox terrier and hedgehog and the flashlight photo of a badger in 1938 (*see p. 14*).

different levels of feeling about our relationships with animals. Recently Eric and his wife Eileen have been devoting much of their energies to rehabilitating injured and abandoned foxes and, in one picture, an obviously well-recuperated orphan has been caught standing on its hind legs behind a camera and seemingly peering through the viewfinder. It is good postcard comedy, with just a touch of forgivable sentimentality. Yet for such bright and insatiably curious mammals (they already muck-in with the domestic round at Badger Cottage) it isn't really such an outlandish or contrived scene. It is the kind of prank wild foxes might pull, if anyone left a camera standing in a field. And, at a more serious level, it is a reminder that Eric's portraits also hint at the views animals hold of *us*. There are few of his images in which some kind of human presence – benign, puzzling, barbarous on occasions – is not implied or reflected.

Eric has never felt tempted to work much beyond the New Forest boundaries (though I suspect his rapport with animals would be the same in Africa or Amazonia), and he may be one of those naturalists, like Gilbert White, whose sensibilities are deepened when they are deliberately confined within an intimately known locality. It would certainly be hard to think of any region of Britain more suited to his particular outlook and talents. The New Forest is a huge and eccentric anomaly, a refuge from the suffocating tameness of much of southern England, yet a place where humans and animals have lived convivially together for centuries. It is the most popular wooded playground in the country, yet has almost nothing in common with the neat and pocket-sized landscapes that are supposed to epitomise our 'rural heritage'. It is in a state of almost permanent siege – split by a dual carriageway whose creation was a national disgrace and squeezed by Southampton's industrial complexes to the east and Bournemouth's ribbon development to the west – yet it still hangs on doggedly as the largest patch of uncultivated lowland landscape in north-west Europe.

It has become customary to trace the survival of this unlikely relic of the medieval landscape back to William the Conqueror, who appropriated the whole of this corner of Hampshire (about 500 square miles then) as a Royal hunting estate. Afforestment had little to do with trees as such, but meant that laws were enacted to conserve cover for game, with the usual result that a brake was put on the advance of cultivation. But the New Forest's mixture of woodland, heath, bog and grassland had been established as a communal source of fuel-wood and grazing long before 1080. It was the soils underlying the Forest which more than any other single factor determined its fate. They are amongst the poorest in this part of England, and even free of Forest Law it is doubtful if they would have seemed worth cultivating until artificial fertilisers became available. As it was, they provided a perfectly satisfactory range of produce under the system known as 'wood-pasture'. This is one of the most ancient and frugal of all agricultural régimes, and was designed to combine the growing of wood and the raising of cattle in the same area of land. The animals fed on the grass and bushes beneath the trees, and foraged acorns and beechmast when these were available. The wood was harvested by the technique of 'pollarding'. Branches were regularly lopped above the level at which the cattle browsed, which ensured that new branches would grow in their place. Pollarding ceased in the Forest at the end of the 17th century, but it has left a record in the characteristically squat and gnarled shapes of the oldest trees.

Both firewood and grazing were common property, and any smallholder who had a cottage or tenement inside the Forest qualified as a 'commoner' and had rights to them. The only way that William's appropriation affected this balanced and equitable system was to add Crown ownership to the already existing list of natural checks and balances.

During the centuries which followed, as the Crown gradually switched its interest from deer to timber, the resolute defence of their respective interests by landowner and commoners ensured that no dramatic changes occurred in the character of the Forest. The Crown attempted to protect the woodland and made some unpopular enclosures for timber plantations. The commoners, represented by their cattle and ponies, grazed back advancing scrub and kept the plains and heaths open. More recently, nature conservationists and the recreational public have also become interested parties, and have successfully prevented the Crown (now represented by the Forestry Commission) from converting the remaining areas of natural woodland ('the Ancient and Ornamental Woodlands') to conifer plantations. None of these compromises are ideal solutions. There are invariably either too many grazing animals to allow the woods to regenerate or too few to keep the heaths open. The commoners wish they could drain more of the bogs and the Forestry Commission that it could extend its fenced enclosures. Yet even when check and balance has occasionally deteriorated into deadlock and cussedness, it has at least kept rushed and ill-considered changes at bay.

This history of organic evolution is one of the reasons the Forest has survived, and also, perhaps, why its remarkable mosaic of habitats has proved so perennially attractive to visual artists. Even in the 18th century, when the whole rural landscape was less disciplined and enclosed, William Gilpin, champion of the cause of Picturesque scenery (and the vicar of Boldre, on the southern edge of the Forest) reckoned that few parts of England

'. . . *afford a greater variety of beautiful landscapes. Its woody scenes, its extended lawns, grassy glades, and vast sweeps of wild country, unlimited by artificial boundaries, together with its river views and distant coasts; are all in a great degree magnificent.*'

The antiquity, the sense of refuge, and above all the wild, unplanned alternations of habitat were repeatedly praised by writers and artists during the 19th and early 20th centuries:

'. . . *as the grand simplicity of such scenery demands – the exquisite subtlety with which nature has blended method and caprice, order and disorder, tenderness and strength, and the exquisite proportion with which nature has during the gliding centuries established between the open spaces – the heaths, lawns, greens, glades and gladeways – and the woods and shaggy woodland, a proportion which no art could reproduce, and invaluable in forming the taste of the observer.*' Catalogue accompanying an exhibition of New Forest paintings, 1875

Small family farmers on the edge of the New Forest were still using ancient methods of sowing corn, *above left*, when Eric came to live in the New Forest in 1936.

Above Family at work, 1937.

Scything oats, *left*, in 1937 on the edge of the New Forest. Note the stooks of corn in distant fields all cut by hand.

Right Small-holder carting corn, 1936.

'The tracks all give far views, over wild foregrounds, to distant cultivation. They reveal the vision of a primeval waste, set in the midst of an older and more fertile formation: of heathlands surrounded by the chalk hills of Dorset, Wilts, and the Isle of Wight.' Heywood Sumner, 1910

'The slopes that connect the moorland with the timbered lowland partake of the vegetation of both, and form a debatable land between them, where descending tongues of heath interpenetrate the advancing wedges of rough woodland. The exquisite interchange of hill and dale, and the random wild-wood characteristic of this intermediate region, give to the New Forest scenery its peculiar beauty.' G. E. Briscoe Eyre, 1871

That notion of the land being 'debatable' comes close to catching what I feel about the Forest myself. It has always seemed an unclaimed, unresolved territory, whose excitement lies, I suspect, quite literally in its boundlessness. There are not only no fences (or very few), but no clear edges to things, and an enticing sense of indefiniteness about the whole place. Everything seems subtly on the move – shifting, merging, shedding, decaying, beginning again. Even the ancient woods are migrating slowly about the Forest, dying back in one patch and advancing in another.

I was dimly aware of this aura of unlimited possibility on my first childhood visit, though uneasy, too. I was with a school scout troop, and went through the small *rite de passage* of spending my first night alone under canvas. I can remember the stifling smell of August bracken, a glimpse of a dark scything falcon – a hobby, I think – but most of all an exhilarating sense of freedom as I hiked along the labyrinth of pony-tracks and valley streams which never seemed to cross a road.

Ever since, the New Forest has provided an infallible release from black

moods and feelings of entrapment. In midsummer dusks I have tiptoed slowly behind nightjars dust-bathing on the heathland tracks and gliding up stiff-winged to keep just a few yards in front of me. In winter I have watched ash-grey hen harriers quartering the woodland edges, over ground crusted with beads of ice. Even a snatched visit on a broken journey can be intoxicating. The rattle of the first cattle grids at Cadnam still makes my spine tingle. Within yards there are glimpses of ancient trees standing, as they do almost nowhere else in Britain, in unpampered grassland; and later, of vistas like that from the high ground near Picket Post, where you can gaze out over ten miles of tousled, unfenced land and wandering animals to the oil refineries on the Solent. There is, in prospects like this, a sense of innocent, almost prelapsarian origins that I suspect is close to the heart of the Forest's appeal.

Eric Ashby began coming to this liberating place when he was a child. He was born in 1918 on the west coast of Cumberland, and spent all his early years in the countryside, including a spell in Lymington close to the New Forest. When he was ten his parents decided on a move to Southsea, for the sake of their children's schooling, and it was here in 1930 that Eric attended a lecture by the pioneer film-maker and explorer Cherry Kearton. From that moment Eric began to dream of making his own photographic record of wildlife in natural habitats. He had already acquired his first camera, an old-style mahogany model, whose plates had to be developed and printed at home. By the time he was sixteen he was taking accomplished photographs of birds. The *Boy's Own Paper* for August 1935 carries Eric's first published work, an article written and illustrated by him on 'Bird Photography – An Ideal Hobby'. It has notes on the building of a hide, and strict instructions about returning nest-sites to the conditions in which they were found.

First published photograph: thrushes in *Boy's Own Paper*, 1935.

His real ambitions lay in the field of moving pictures, and later that year he managed to save enough money – £6.10s – to buy a second-hand 16mm Ensign. ·Soon he was filming house-martins on the Isle of Wight. But it was to be another twenty-five years before Eric's films received any kind of public recognition. Before that, Eric's father died in 1932. He had suspected that farming was the only suitable occupation for his country-loving sons, and the family, still thinking in terms of a farming future, moved temporarily into a cottage on the edge of the New Forest while they searched for an affordable holding. But there was nothing suitable, and in 1939 they had to settle for a property in Devon. It was an 86 acre mixed farm with stock, corn, potatoes and vegetables, and to Eric's delight – he had photographed his first badger just before leaving the

Above Hares boxing. This is usually caused by the doe objecting to early advances from the buck.

Above left Eric's first flashlight photo of a badger emerging from its sett, 9 March 1938.

Left House-martins at Badger Cottage.

Forest – both a badger sett and a fox earth. It also had 500 free-range poultry, and Eric recalls with some pride that, thanks to his understanding of animal behaviour, they did not lose a single bird to foxes during fourteen years of farming.

In 1953 Eric returned to the New Forest, settled at Linwood and began accumulating the footage that was eventually to form the basis of *The Unknown Forest*. Badgers – a passion ever since he had heard about the cruelties of badger-baiting as a boy – were his favourite subject, and his early pictures of them were an extraordinary achievement. They were taken in daylight with a home-made kapok-lined 'blimp' to dull the noise of the camera, and were almost certainly the first 'natural' films to be taken of wild badgers.

Eric's breakthrough happened almost by chance in 1958. The BBC's Natural History Unit at Bristol were anxious to broaden the scope and appeal of their programmes, and were casting about for original British film-makers with a potential for reaching a mass audience. A producer had read an article by Eric in *The Countryman*, and travelled down to the Forest to view his material. So it was that in the October of that year, Christopher Parsons, later head of the Unit, sat in a viewing room in Bristol, transfixed by the first close-up pictures he or anyone else had seen of wild badgers digging, playing and feeding. Eric was given a contract immediately, and spent 1959 filming additional sequences. *The Unknown Forest* was screened on 19th January 1961, and had an overwhelmingly favourable public response.

Over the years that followed Eric made a score of films for the BBC, all photographed in southern England, and most of them concentrating on the Forest and its large mammals. In these, as in his still pictures, he has worked to an unwavering set of principles. He has never faked continuity to create a better story-line, or used tame animals posing as wild ones. He has never employed trick photography and refers dismissively to some modern initiatives in this direction as '*un*-natural history films'. Instead Eric relies on intuition, patience and sheer fieldcraft, sometimes tracking animals downwind for hours before setting up his camera. Ever since that first foray in *Boy's Own Paper* he has insisted that the welfare of his subjects comes first. He has told me of the time he was filming a nesting Dartford warbler – one of Britain's rarest resident birds which has its last precarious stronghold on the Forest heaths. He allowed himself one hour in the hide (a long time for a bird but short for a photographer), while Eileen sat in a parked car nearby, flicking ostentatiously through the pages of a book to distract any passers-by.

But Eric's perseverance has been rewarded, with a remarkable collection of insights into the lives of ordinary creatures and with a glimpse of a world where the barrier between humans and nature has, for a moment, been lowered. One of his most telling and endearing pictures (facing p. 1) is of a group of three different species of mammal consorting in the garden of Badger Cottage. There is Eric himself, remote control shutter in hand; the immense and imperturbable cat, Ginger, a stray who had taken up residence in Eric's badger sett; and, emerging from the sett just a few yards away, a wild badger.

Eric's art is essentially that of a story-teller. Although many of his Forest landscapes are striking compositions, what makes his animal pictures so compelling is the hint of past and future events uncoiling from them. Like all fine photographs they do not 'freeze' time, but admit its passing. And an important part of their narrative concerns Eric's relationship with his subjects. Many of his strongest portraits show animals looking directly at the camera – and not always because they are unaware of its presence. They have captured that special moment when a human and a wild creature have accepted each other's presence.

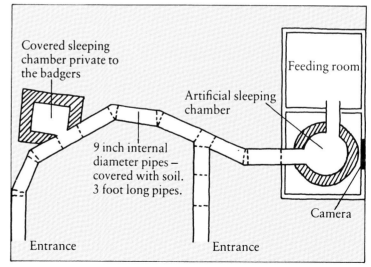

Above In the badger sett. The photo on the *left* shows a rare glimpse of a sow suckling her three cubs.

Right Plan of the artificial badger sett. The pipes enter a bank and are below ground but enter the viewing area at ground level.

Covered sleeping chamber private to the badgers

Artificial sleeping chamber

Feeding room

9 inch internal diameter pipes – covered with soil. 3 foot long pipes.

Camera

Entrance

Entrance

In 1975 Eric began building an artificial badger sett in his garden, in order to have better opportunities to film the animals at close quarters. (It is now nicknamed 'the film sett'.) This is as close as he has ever come to intervening in his subjects' lives.

It was a complicated project (see p. 17). He excavated a series of trenches about 80 yards from the natural sett on the edge of his lawn and filled them with wide concrete pipes to act as tunnels. They led to a glass-fronted chamber under the garden shed. Many months later a family of badgers moved in, and Eric – gradually accustoming them to artificial light – was able to take the first-ever film of wild mammals underground. There was no interference with the badgers' lifestyles beyond the provision of a few pounds of scraps every day.

In 1987 Eric was preparing to make another film based on the badgers, which had now started to breed in the artificial sett. But early that year his property was invaded by the local foxhunt. The hounds ran riot across his garden, pounding the soft edges of the natural sett entrances, and causing all the badgers (including the pregnant females) to desert. Eric has always opposed the activities of the three New Forest Hunts, which collectively mount 165 meets a year in the Forest. But on this occasion they had violated not only his feelings but the relationships he had been building up with a specific family of badgers over many years, and he decided to apply for an injunction forbidding foxhunters to trespass on his two and a half acres.

It was a brave act, made at some personal cost. The case attracted much publicity and the attention of pro-hunt extremists. Eric began to receive anonymous communications. One night he found his garage broken into, and a dead fox with its face smashed in lying on the lawn. In January 1988, when the badger family had started to move back, someone drenched the natural sett with Renardine, an agricultural chemical used to repel foxes and badgers (from chicken runs and the like), though supposedly regarded as unethical by the hunting community. Again the badgers deserted.

There is no evidence that the New Forest Hunts were involved in any of these witless acts of vandalism. But after Eric had successfully applied for his injunction they chose a curious way of complying. Instead of simply declaring his property out of bounds (the usual procedure) they built a permanent 6 foot high, animal-proof fence along 300 yards of his northern boundary. On hunting days an electric fence is strung along most of the rest. The fences keep the hounds out, but also all the other wild animals that share Badger Cottage, including a herd of fallow deer which, Eric says, 'used to feed on our land every day, often lying down in front of our windows'. The fence was erected by hunt members, and *Hounds* magazine, thanking the 'ever-faithful band of Foot-floggers', christened it 'stage one of Stalag Ashby'.

I thought of this peculiarly tasteless analogy as I sat in the garden of Badger Cottage on an autumn afternoon, romping with the orphan foxes (see pp. 20–21), and marvelling at how Eric had kept his tolerant outlook in the face of such provocation. In response there has been a hint of changing attitudes in the Hunt, and the new Joint Master is suggesting a no-go area around Eric's land.

I spent most of the next day wandering in the Forest, and thinking about the grim symbolism of that fence around Badger Cottage, and I realised more acutely than ever before how much I (and all lovers of the place, I suspect) treasured that sense of having free run of such a vast area of wild country. It was a fine autumn day, with a soft breeze coming off the sea, and made for walking. I picked my way through damp valleys where the whole air was scented with bog myrtle, glimpsed a kingfisher darting through a tunnel of blackberries over Linford Brook, scrambled about among an immense willow brought down in

Above Vicky was brought to the Ashbys at about 8 weeks old, suffering from mange and rickets. She had to have a shampoo every five days for five weeks which she suffered without complaint, playing happily with her towel later.

Left A recuperating fox at Badger Cottage, with Ginger.

Foxes at Badger Cottage.

the 1987 gale, and already bristling with new green shoots along the whole length of its trunk.

Serendipity comes easily here. On a high heath near Bolderwood I was looking out towards the unfenced woods of Bushy Bratley when I saw a pert, dusky-plumaged warbler darting about between the gorse clumps. It flicked its tail up on landing and even from a distance I could make out its flanks shining the colour of heather flowers in the sun. It was a Dartford warbler, the species which Eric had photographed on the nest all those years ago, now the Forest's rarest small bird and the first I had ever seen. They are usually the shyest of birds, but true to the spirit of the place that day, this one sported about in the open for a full quarter of an hour. Through my binoculars I could see its brilliant red eye and steel-grey back. And I saw one other extraordinary thing: the air between us was full of strings of translucent gossamer, and the warbler was feasting on money spiders, dangled out of the sky.

My thanks go out to Eric for that day. He has helped educate the eyes and sensibilities of all of us, and in this corner of England has been a stalwart defender of the wild creatures themselves. As I write, the future of the New Forest and its creatures looks rather better than it has for some time. The prospect of oil-drilling still hovers ominously in the background, but the plans for a new coal-fired power station at nearby Fawley have been withdrawn, and those for a Lyndhurst bypass defeated. As for hunting, it seems increasingly of a piece with these other City-based threats, with their fashionable ethos of aggressive self-interest, and I believe that in due course it will be seen off as a graceless throwback, with no place in the modern Forest.

What the New Forest can show us — and what Eric Ashby's pictures celebrate — is the power of wild creatures to elevate and inform the human spirit, and the possibility of a contract between humans, nature and the land.

THE
FOREST YEAR

❧ SPRING ❧

In Spring the New Forest re-awakens gently at first. After a dull spell, suddenly the sunlight is brighter and warmer. The first brimstone butterfly is seen and we are always cheered to find the first celandine in flower. The early hazel catkins might have appeared in January but these were soon blackened with frost; now severe frost is unlikely and hardy plants are growing without check. At last the woods and gardens resound with joyous bird song.

This is the time when cameras come out in earnest. Soon it is hard to know which way to turn; I am so busy that Spring goes far too quickly. Frogs spawn rather late in the Forest, often in March, but they are not very prolific as the poor acid soil does not provide an abundance of food. Some early birds are nesting, the earliest of all, the crossbill, a bird whose numbers fluctuate in this part of the world, nests high in the conifers as early as February, its food being the seeds found in fir cones which its crossed bill is able to extract.

The first fox cubs are often seen in the second half of April when four or five weeks old, staying out only for a few minutes at first, while the vixen suckles them, as it begins to be a little cramped down below with growing cubs.

People like to walk the Forest streams but not many will notice the more unusual life underwater. Here and there shoals of small fish are obvious but it needs more careful search to see newts displaying in April and brook lampreys moving stones with their sucker mouths to create a clear space for spawning, so that the eggs will not be swept away in the current. How much more rewarding to both photographer and viewer to film this activity taking place in its natural habitat instead of in the artificial conditions of an aquarium.

On warm sunny mornings in Spring many animals like to sunbathe, often choosing the same spot on succeeding days. One needs to move carefully and silently, so as not to disturb the deer, fox, bird or other creature taking advantage of the warmth. On south-facing banks an adder might be sunning itself, but when the weather is too hot it will disappear before mid-morning. It has probably been hibernating in a hole by the old fence posts. The usual colour of adders is rather dull, with black zig-zag markings running along their backs; more unusual are those predominantly red, cream or black.

Even badgers sometimes leave a heap of bedding near one of their sett entrances and, on rare occasions, have been seen asleep in the Spring sun.

Many years ago in the 1950s when certain badger setts were undisturbed, I was able to film an adult with her cubs in the evening sunlight during the third week of April. I was delighted as this was almost certainly the first film ever taken of a badger family in colour.

Spring is one of the times we might see unusual birds, making their way north to nest. Some, there is no doubt, stay and nest in secluded and secret places – such as a pair of pied flycatchers one year and a little ringed plover another. Hoopoe and golden oriole are recorded only as visitors and yet I heard the latter singing strongly in the Forest once. I like to think it may have stayed. The beauty of the Forest is its wildness: much wildlife goes unrecorded and therefore safe from fatal disturbance. We hope that readers will help to keep it so.

The nightingale is unfortunately rare in the Forest. As a result of hard browsing by the larger animals the undergrowth in most places is unsuitable for the bird and few stay to nest. Before 1939 I remember almost every little coppice outside the bounds resounded to a nightingale's song, but not now, partly at least because the hazel understory is no longer cut for hurdle-making, and thus the woodland is too overgrown and dark and the ground beneath, cut off from the light, is bare.

Blackthorn flowers rather late in the Forest. Here the
picture is enlivened by a visiting blue tit.

Towards the end of April most of the fallow bucks will have cast their antlers and the new season's antlers will have started to grow. They will also be losing their long, dark winter coats, revealing a bright, sleek, dappled dress. Jackdaws and starlings searching for soft material to line their nests find the cast-off fur ideal and will pull lumps off from the backs of the bucks.

One of the advantages of having fallow bucks in our garden, treating our land as a sanctuary from the dangers of the Forest and confident that we would not harm them, has been that we could study them closely. Running from the nearby Forest they would often settle down a few feet from our windows. The soft purring noise they made while snoozing on a hot afternoon, so quiet it can only be heard near at hand, was surprising and interesting. As soon as they left our property they returned to being shy, unapproachable wild animals.

We always look forward to the arrival of wheatears, birds which nest in rabbit burrows. One regular site is a drainpipe used by birds and rabbits. Wishing to see that the pipe was clear of obstructions, I put my arm down on one occasion and found a monster toad! Even the humble rabbit is worth stopping to watch, perhaps feeding or sunbathing by day, but active in early morning and evening. Strangely, perhaps, mice sometimes share their homes with larger animals, particularly in woodland where they can be heard foraging amongst the dry leaves, making as much noise as the larger occupants. Once we saw a beetle hauling a rabbit pellet backwards, just like a badger dragging a bundle of bedding.

Right An inquisitive fox cub outside its den, deep in the New Forest.

Left The shy roe doe, recognisable by her small size – about 2ft at the shoulder – and lack of tail.

Above Most roe kids are born in May, the earliest of the young deer to be seen – if you are very lucky.

Right Young roe buck in Spring, his thick winter coat starting to be shed around the shoulders.

Above Fallow deer visitors to our windblown orchard.

Right A 3-year-old sika stag – one of the present population living in the south of the New Forest. These are said to be Japanese deer, descendants of four which escaped from the Beaulieu Estate in 1904–5.

Above Wood sorrel flowering amongst the primroses and wood anemones in open woodland at Badger Cottage.

Left Springtime in Mark Ash, one of the most popular of the Ancient and Ornamental woodlands.

Above left One of the first heralds of Spring, the lesser celandine.

Above Young rabbits sunning themselves on the white sandy soil outside their home.

Left A rare pink variety of wood anemone.

Right Where two streams join at Queen's Bower, near Brockenhurst.

Left Early purple orchid amongst primroses in our woodland garden. When we arrived at Badger Cottage in 1953 under the oak and ash trees was a cover of old hazel, so thick that nothing grew on the Forest floor. We cleared the bushes, digging out the stumps, rotavated the ground and planted grass seeds. Over the years a thick cover of primroses has grown with a scattering of early purple and twayblade orchids.

Right A New Forest vixen suckling her cubs while one reaches up in greeting. Our tame foxes greet visitors in the same way, reading them with their sense of smell like a book.

Left Vicky at about 8 weeks old, and, *right*, as she is now.

It was almost by accident that we have been keeping rescued foxes since 1985 when we agreed to keep a friend's cub while she went on holiday, and ended up giving 'Tiger' a permanent home. Tiny bottle-fed cubs can never be set free and it is virtually impossible to find anyone to look after them . . .

Jack and Jill came to Badger Cottage at about 6 weeks old. A bulldozer had been driven through their earth, killing the vixen, but the driver kindly took the cubs to the RSPCA. Fortunately Sheba, a resident vixen at Badger Cottage, adopted them.

Left A frog in late Spring.

Above Frogs spawning when the weather warms up in March.

Right Bog bean – a flower to be seen near the edges of some Forest pools.

Above left Safe from predators, a spotted flycatcher regularly rears young on a shelf specially fixed in one of our sheds.

Above right Lapwings, or peewits, come to the boggy parts of the Forest in Spring to nest.

Right Great spotted woodpecker arriving with food for its young in an ash tree. The nest hole was excavated some years ago and has been a nest site for both woodpeckers and starlings.

Old and storm damaged trees, a speciality of the old 'New' Forest, provide homes for many birds such as this successfully reared family of kestrels. Bats, bees and many insects also find sanctuary in these trees.

Left In a remote spot a patch of wild daffodils is found safe and untouched.

Right Green-winged orchid in old pasture in our garden: once growing in profusion in unploughed fields, now most have been ploughed or fertilised and smothered by the resulting rank grass. Our small sanctuary can boast four kinds of orchid.

❦ SUMMER ❦

There seems to be no dividing line between Spring and Summer. Perhaps the first really hot day decides the issue. The year is rushing on far too fast.

During many years of amateur photography from boyhood onwards, one recalls interesting incidents, some sad, some amusing. Mammals are the most difficult subjects: they have an extremely good sense of smell and hearing which most birds do not have. Therefore the wind must be blowing from the animal to you and a quiet-running camera is essential.

I made a sound-proof box for my cine camera with long focus lens, which looked very much like a coffin. At the time I was making many visits to a particular badger sett to get the sequence I wanted. But unbeknown I had been watched by the police, carrying this suspicious-looking load. One afternoon the badgers were already foraging, when out of the shadows walked a constable talking loudly as he approached. I lifted my hand for silence and pointed to the badgers. He was staggered, saying: 'Badgers, well I'm blowed – are they yours?'

We are pleased the police are so observant and hope it involves the guilty as well as the innocent. Once there was a robbery in Salisbury and we had pulled off the road to change a film in our van. The police who spotted us thought we were sorting out the loot.

Egg collectors can be a menace, mainly because they go for the rare and interesting species. One day we were walking to a nightjar's nest to check it. In the distance a man and woman were walking a gravel track; nothing unusual in this, but when we revisited the nest, the eggs had been replaced by two pebbles and the bird had deserted. Even a certain bird photographer might have done just as much damage in a different way. This man had cut the growth above the nest of a red-backed shrike which contained young, replacing the original cover with fragile greenery which shrivelled in the sun, leaving the youngsters suffering severely from the heat. They would not have survived. I covered the nest with a conifer branch which provided permanent shade. Red-backed shrikes no longer nest in the Forest nor does the Montagu's harrier which also suffered from interference. Of course, the deterioration in the weather (particularly in Spring it has been, on average, wetter and colder in the Forest for the last fifteen to twenty years) is largely responsible for the reduction in numbers of some forms of Forest wildlife. Disturbance and robbery must have hastened the demise of the shrikes who depend on a plentiful supply of large insects such as bees. Even the casual observer will have noticed the reduction in the number of butterflies.

Wild natural behaviour can be seen in the cattle on the Forest with their calves. Quite often an 'auntie' cow will be observed with several calves in attendance. 'Auntie' has taken on the task of baby-sitting while the mothers wander off feeding.

All Spring and Summer while the fallow bucks' antlers are growing, swarms of flies cause a real nuisance to the poor animals, clustering around parts of the new growth, particularly if the velvet covering the soft growing horn has been slightly damaged and is bleeding. Starlings and pied wagtails help by picking off flies from head and antlers, while the buck holds his head still. Meanwhile a young wagtail might be perched on the buck's back waiting to be fed.

The New Forest consists of a great variety of soils, some wet and heavy clay, some dry sand and gravel, all poor acid soil. There are large areas of enclosed woodlands (called Inclosures) worked commercially by the Forestry Commission, both deciduous and conifer. Probably the most obviously unique feature of the New Forest is the natural open woodland areas which are called 'Ancient

Above left Ponies graze right up to the boundary of Badger Cottage.

Above right The unique character of the unfenced open Forest has been formed by the continuous grazing and browsing of the hardy ponies and cattle.

and Ornamental' and are kept from becoming a jungle by grazing and browsing animals. There is also a vast area of heathland and bog. Because of all this great variety of habitat the Forest contains a large number of species of wildlife, though they are increasingly thin on the ground, from the very small to the largest of our land mammals – the red stag.

Owing to the poor acid soil conditions, food for such animals as badgers is hard to come by. Worms for example, the staple food of badgers on good soil, are fairly scarce. Therefore it is imperative that badgers are as undisturbed as possible to allow them as much foraging time as they need. Yet the badger population since the Second World War has declined drastically, I have often said by at least half, though it could be as much as three-quarters. Because of the poor supply of food, the Forest was one of the few places where badgers could in the past be seen out in full daylight. I used to see badgers foraging in mid-morning and early afternoon during the Summer when the population was much higher. Now it is very rare to see one before late evening. Only where the Forest adjoins private land are the animals doing well and this is where food is plentiful and they need not emerge early.

Several reasons have been put forward for their decline. Some say it is the increase in the area of conifers, but, according to the recent New Forest Review, the extent of conifer plantation is little greater than it was fifty years ago, reducing the food supply only slightly overall. In any case, badgers have declined just as seriously in hardwood woodland. There has certainly been a greater number of visitors who are alleged to cause disturbance. But even this argument does not hold water, as the Forest has been barred to motor vehicles for some years and therefore remote setts are unlikely to be disturbed by visitors any more than previously. Also, at the time of year when visitors are badger-watching, the cubs are active and can move to another sett if unduly disturbed.

Above left Up to 22 fallow bucks used to enter our garden, often lying down peacefully to chew the cud within a few feet of our kitchen window – until the local foxhunt erected a 6ft fence along our boundary.

Above right Our ginger tom cat loved to spend time with Tiger the dog fox. Foxes are normally wary of cats who are well able to protect themselves should they have to.

As a boy I was much concerned on reading Henry Williamson's story of Brock the badger, a story of digging and baiting with terriers, which although now illegal still goes on. Perhaps this is why the badger is one of my favourite animals.

One of the animals featured in my first television programme in 1961 was the badger, an animal almost unseen then by the general public.

Many of the programmes that followed included badger material, until in 1974, I was told the BBC could not consider any more unless I could go underground to film their private lives. I explained that this would be impossible: any interference with their home would cause badgers to desert, and I could not consider using tame animals.

However, I knew that badgers were not so shy *away* from their home. I thought it worth trying to attract them to an artificial sett. In the wild, badgers have a main breeding sett with small outlying setts near feeding grounds where they would stay for a few days according to seasonal food supplies. This is what I hoped to create – an outlying sett next to a never-failing tree of plenty, so that I could film natural activity in a chamber made to look like the real thing.

Left and right Rare pictures of wild badger families in the Forest.

Early in 1975 I dug trenches and laid pipes. Soon after the feeding room was opened, I disturbed a badger feeding at night. Then came the problem of conditioning the animals to light. I had to start with 5 watts and gradually increase the strength over several weeks. By June 19th, using a 500 watt lamp gradually turned up to full power, I took an experimental shot of an adult and three cubs sleeping.

Thus I was able to see and film natural badger behaviour underground for the first time: play, mutual grooming, scent marking, bringing in bedding and bedmaking, cubs suckling and just sleeping.

Above right An adult badger entering the sleeping and photographic chamber, known as the 'film sett'.

Left and right Well grown cubs at play.

Left The wild gladiolus, always under the protection of bracken, is the plant speciality of the New Forest, growing nowhere else in Britain.

Right This butterfly orchid has survived here under cover of bracken where it is less likely to be eaten or trodden by grazing animals.

Above Young tawny owl resting, after leaving the nest the previous night.

Left Female tawny owl ready to leave the nest in search of prey.

Right Looking to see if the coast is clear. Tawny owls do hunt by day as these photographs show. The female owl returned with food for the youngster at 4.15pm, rested on the edge of the nest hole and then flew away – all in broad daylight.

Left Grey squirrel, the mammal most often seen in the Forest, disliked by foresters because it feeds on leading shoots of trees and strips the bark of chestnuts. In its favour, it also eats the seeds in fir cones, reducing the spread of self-sown pine trees.

Right The best loved woodland birds are surely the woodpeckers, three of which occur in the New Forest. Here the great spotted woodpecker is searching for grubs in an oak tree.

During the summer many silver-washed fritillary butterflies are seen, *right*, as well as speckled woods, *above left*, and commas, *above right*.

Left Practically no plants grew in this piece of woodland before the undergrowth was cleared. Now there is a mass of foxgloves and other small plants.

Above A yearling fallow buck, called a pricket. Fallow deer are the most common deer – easily identified by their long tails.

Right Full grown fallow buck in summer coat, antlers in velvet and nearly full size. In late August the velvet will be rubbed off on springy branches.

Above A sitting woodcock is so well camouflaged that it could be stepped on! A bird more often heard than seen in the late evening as it flies around its territory – on its 'roding' flight.

Left A heather path – bell heather and ling.

Left Pond life in the New Forest.

Right After 2 or more years underwater, in its larval state, a dragonfly nymph emerges, and in a short while the adult breaks out of the case – a beautiful creature quite different from the one which emerged from the mud of the pond. The New Forest can boast 29 of the 39 species of dragonfly which breed in Britain.

I was lucky in photographing these sand lizards (male *left*, female *above right*), a very rare reptile in the New Forest. In other places, notably Dorset, their sandy habitats are liable to be chosen as building sites – here in the Forest planning permission is more difficult to obtain.

Right The adder (or viper) is our only poisonous snake, not often seen as it is very sensitive to approaching footsteps.

Above One has to be about in the early morning to see the dew-soaked cobwebs in summer.

Left and right The sundew grows in acid bogs and wet heathland. The plant obtains its nitrogen requirements by trapping insects and digesting their nutrients.

One day a fox cub was brought to our door wrapped in a towel; it had been injured by a fox terrier. Our vet gave it treatment. It was quiet during the day, feeding quite well, but next morning the bathroom was in a mess. The following morning even more destruction had occurred, and the only thing to do was to put it out in a well-fenced fox pen. Within a couple of hours it had escaped. We were most distressed – for the first time we had let a cub down. But we need not have worried. Earlier in the year we had set free two wary and nocturnal vixens and now they were picking up food and taking it down to the corner of the field where the badger sett is situated. A wild fox was doing the same. Nothing strange in that we thought. Then one day I found the injured cub sleeping outside the lower hole of the sett. Later I managed to take the *photo on the right*. Months later he is still around, a healthy wild fox. The moral is, of course, don't pick up an apparently abandoned animal: its chances of survival are much better if left alone, unless, of course, there is an obvious injury needing attention.

Left Young or old, foxes are always playful.

❦ AUTUMN ❦

Autumn can be a beautiful time in the Forest, with mellow sunlight and little wind, interspersed with spells of rain and gales which make us appreciate the fine days when they come. Early in September most of the fallow bucks have shed the velvet covering which was protecting their growing antlers during the previous months. Magpies love to pull off this blood-covered skin which presumably contains some feeding value. The bucks don't object: their horns are now hard bone and have no feeling. October is the time of the fallow rut, the breeding season; at this time the bucks are given a brief respite from the New Forest buck hunt. Early in the month the bucks leave their Summer feeding grounds and make their way to their breeding areas, sometimes miles away. Arriving at the often ancient rutting stands they scrape hollows in the ground around a small area, sometimes in the very same scrapes as the previous year. They rub their antlers on nearby bushes and young trees, leaving the scent from their forehead glands as a warning to other bucks wishing to occupy the site. Fights for the mastery of the stand often occur, frequently in the early morning. The calling of the bucks to attract the does echoes throughout the woodlands, coming to a peak towards the end of October. The nearest I can describe the call is a frequent but short, loud snore. This attracts many does, fawns and bucks to the area. Photography of this activity in wild deer is very difficult – any outlying animal will easily spot or scent you and alert the others, even before you can get within range.

The breeding season of the red deer is also in the Autumn but earlier than the fallow. These deer, the largest of our land mammals, like to wallow in mud and water. One year I found an old bomb crater showing signs of being used as a wallow, with a convenient tree nearby suitable for a camera. I hid up the tree on several early mornings without any luck, though the deer were not far away. Then on one occasion, making my way to the site, I was delayed by a Forester and, arriving late, I climbed the tree, fixed the tripod head, but then could not move for some time because of the arrival of several red hinds who promptly wallowed. The cine camera was down below at the foot of the tree! One hind was nearly submerged in muddy water and the others were splashing the water high in the air, making a beautiful picture against the morning sun. Such is the frequent frustration of wildlife photography. One sees many more exciting things than one can ever record on film. On another occasion a stag was approaching another wallow, and I had the camera set up all ready, when a walker wearing a bright white shirt came up behind, asking politely, 'Have you managed to get some good pictures?' I never succeeded in filming reds wallowing.

But by dint of much persistence from September to November I have managed to shoot a great deal of footage of Sika stags wallowing. These deer don't roar or snore at rutting time, but give out a loud whistle, three or four times in succession – enough to make one jump if near at hand – and one may also hear a loud groan. These strange deer from the Far East also wallow in peaty mud and then look black and quite sinister. One shot I filmed was the longest ever shown on any BBC *Look* programme. The stag came to the wallow, had a long, long drink, before getting down into the muddy hollow, rubbing his neck, smoothing and scent-marking the edge of the wallow, then getting up and leaving. A nice example of animal behaviour. All the time I was on tenter-hooks hoping the film would not run out before the end of the action!

The abundance of fruit on bush and tree attracts the Autumn migrants. Even at night redwings can be heard calling as they fly over the cottage. Many birds

Above Ginger sunning himself in our woodland garden on a misty Autumn morning.

Right A wild fox coming for scraps watched by Ginger, our cat. Ginger was a stray living on our badger sett where he was very wary and wild, diving down into the sett whenever I approached. We tamed him and found he loved to watch all the wildlife visiting Badger Cottage.

and mammals are helped by a plentiful acorn, chestnut and beechmast year and have a good breeding season the following Spring. A poor crop results in few rodents and fewer young owls. The not very frugal squirrels start on the hazel nuts at the end of July, long before the nut has grown to a reasonable size, so that all have been cleared by the time they should be ready for harvesting.

Redwings, fieldfares and other members of the thrush family feed on the berries of holly, hawthorn and rowan. It does worry us when lorry loads of holly berries are stripped from the bushes for the Christmas trade leaving very little for the birds. Conservation seems to be word but not deed in this Forest which should surely be run with concern for wildlife as the main priority.

The first week of November is usually the best time to see the famous Autumn colours. Given good weather and provided you choose the areas of beech trees, the visit should prove well worthwhile.

Ivy provides the last nectar of the season, attracting insects of all kinds, including red admiral butterflies, which, given warm sunny weather, can be seen up to the end of October and even in early November. A bush covered with flowering ivy can be really humming with insects and any small bird will quickly find a satisfying meal. Under these mild conditions the odd dragonfly may be seen hunting for insects, and at dusk bats will be active and tawny owls are particularly noisy, as this year's youngsters stake out their territory. The plaintive Autumn song of the robin, which fits so well with the time of falling leaves, will be heard, and the clarion song of the missel thrush reminds us of Spring.

Right Fallow buck in the garden on a misty morning.

Right A New Forest fallow buck with his new season antlers fully grown ready for the October rut.

Left A master buck on his rutting stand in late October – a curious young buck looks on.

Left Butcher's broom, an uncommon plant found in old woodland in Southern England.

Right The colourful jay, the oak tree planter. In the Autumn acorns are picked from the trees or from the ground, often six or so at a time, and packed into its crop. The acorns are later regurgitated, a hole dug, and the seeds buried. In spots up to half-a-mile away from the tree, young oaks can grow should the jay, mice or squirrel not find their hidden treasure.

Above Roman Bridge.

Left One of the most beautiful and yet common shrubs of the Forest is the blackthorn – a mass of white flowers in Spring and fruits in Autumn, collected by many to make sloe gin or wine.

Above The New Forest is well known for its great variety of fungi. The fly agaric (*Amanita muscaria*) is one of the most striking. Albertus Magnus in the 13th century recommended it, broken up in milk, as a fly killer.

Right See overleaf.

Left A Forest bye-road in the early morning.

Right The Ancient and Ornamental Woods of the Forest have the minimum interference from foresters, but undergrowth is kept down by ponies, cattle and deer, resulting in picturesque views from all directions.

Page 101 Too many acorns are poisonous to ponies and cattle and so permission is given for pigs to be set free to forage during the 'Pannage Season'. On the other hand, various animals need acorns to survive the winter – deer, badgers, squirrels, some birds such as jays and, last but not least, mice and voles; and they are essential as the main food of tawny owls who have a poor breeding season after a poor acorn crop.

❦ WINTER ❦

Whatever the weather, in Winter the New Forest has a charm all its own. The trees having shed their leaves and with the dead bracken beaten down by rain, the scenes in the deciduous woods are almost unique. These woods are more open than those outside the Forest where grazing and browsing animals rarely enter. The clearings in the woodlands and the open grassland by the streams contribute to the picturesque character of the Forest; the scene changes at every turn. This is the best time of year to see deer without the obstruction of foliage, whether from car or on a cross-country walk.

If you are very fortunate, you may see a hen harrier quartering the open heathland or even a short-eared owl flying low over the ground in search of prey, this being a daylight-loving owl. Another regular visitor to the Forest is the great grey shrike, which looks very striking perched high on a streamside bush with its light-coloured plumage standing out against the dark heather hillside. More than once we have had reports of nutcrackers in a Forest garden, or foxes raiding litter bins at picnic sites. In January news reaches us of foxes hunting in packs. This is a misunderstanding, an example of how an observer can be quite wrong in an interpretation of wildlife activity. This month is the main breeding season of foxes and a vixen in season can be followed by several dog foxes, looking like a hunting pack. Nor are foxes particularly hungry during hard weather, as weakly or dead prey is more easily found at this time.

We are always on the look-out for anything unusual to record on film. Any of the commoners' animals which die in the Forest is normally cleared away but once when we found a pony carcase partly eaten in the snow, we thought it was ideal to hide and watch for any scavenger. Magpies soon appeared and after a long and cold wait, a fox trotted up to have a snack. A really wild scene on this snowy day.

Ever since I started photography, I have been experimenting and making gadgets which might be helpful in this hobby. A few years ago I wanted to film animals at night picked up in the headlights of our van. In addition to the normal lamps I added a pair of halogen spotlights and, loading the camera with highly sensitive film, we drove around, switching on the extra lamps when a possible subject was seen. The fun started when the vehicle began to fill with smoke, causing panic! Something had been wired up incorrectly. No harm had been done but the film results were very under-exposed and useless. Only when the subject was very close was there enough light. Nowadays a video camera would have produced satisfactory results.

The winter weather provides plenty of variety and interest. Water lies everywhere for most of the winter but the scene changes when frost grips the land or snow turns the woods into fairyland. One need never be bored; in fact the days are far too short, with more than enough to do to occupy our time.

Badgers can mate at any time during the year and, because of delayed implantation, cubs are not born until the following year, usually in February. Badgers are highly-strung creatures and are therefore very liable to stress caused by any disturbance, particularly at the time of the implantation period in December and during the following few weeks, until after the cubs are born. Before birth cubs can be re-absorbed, and, after birth, cubs might be eaten if they are disturbed or the mother becomes agitated.

Naturally, therefore, we are particularly concerned in the winter about the devastation to badger setts by the foxhunt's practice of earth-stopping. Sett entrances are blocked with soil on hunting days to prevent any hunted fox from seeking haven, so that the quarry has to keep running to provide 'sport' for the

Above Like dogs, our foxes love to play after a snowfall, though thankfully this does not often occur in the South of England.

Right Sheba is well insulated against the winter cold.

riders. Up to the early 1960s there was very little sett-stopping in our part of the Forest, otherwise I could not have filmed badgers in full daylight for the BBC programmes. Now sett-stopping can occur as frequently as three times a month.

Severe and continuous disturbance such as this has a lasting effect on animal activity, I believe for the animal's lifetime, and eventually can be inborn in the offspring. We have seen this inherited fear in our hand-reared fox cubs from two days old when later they hear the sound of distant hounds or shod horses on the road, whereas they don't mind the barking of ordinary dogs.

Setts are sometimes disturbed in Summer, of course. On one occasion one of the best active setts was visited by a party of children headed by a teacher who should have kept the children from approaching too near. Child footprints were all over the earth at the entrances, the soil must have been impregnated with human scent and also the occupants would have smelt and heard the party above. The sett was later deserted. This is not serious in Summer when cubs are active and can be moved by the parents to a nearby empty sett. Whereas in Winter, when all setts are blocked, the animals have nowhere uncontaminated to find sanctuary and peace.

When I am monitoring setts in Winter, I find some which should have twenty or more entrances open, with only two or three in use, the rest still blocked, the soil muddy and wet – a most depressing sight. Air-flow is reduced below ground, producing unhealthy damp conditions, lowering resistance to disease.

It must surely be undisputed that New Forest wildlife should be given the utmost protection. The New Forest Review Group was set up by the Forestry Commission in 1987 and agreed in its draft recommendation regarding fox hunting: 'In order to afford greater protection to the precarious badger population, digging and the use of terriers by the New Forest Hounds should not be permitted.' This seemed a great step forward but now in 1989 the latest news is

Badger Cottage in winter isolation.

I cut holly branches for the fallow deer who appreciate this extra food and the calf-rearing nuts placed on the ground.

that this move to improve the welfare of badgers, and at the same time avoid cruelty to foxes, has been reversed. Should this barbarous practice continue after all our hopes of its being stopped, I am sure the vast majority of Forest residents will be horrified, particularly as the Nature Conservancy Council has for nearly thirty years asked for the banning of this cruel and destructive activity as well as a ban on the blocking of setts.

Perhaps the powers that be ought to remember the words of St Francis of Assisi: 'Not to hurt our humble brethren is our first duty to them, but to stop there is not enough. We have a higher mission – to be of service to them whenever they require it.'

Above left Cock chaffinch.

Above right A cheeky blue tit.

Left Hips and holly berries provide useful winter rations for birds and mice.

Above Roe buck and doe, caught feeding on a winter morning.

Right There are only a few red deer in the Forest, nearly all to the south of the A31.

Left Fallow bucks are adept at browsing on holly, ivy and various shoots as high as they can reach.

Above Another winter scene in Badger Cottage's woodland garden.

Right When all else fails ponies feed on holly and gorse shoots, which are actually far more nutritious than winter grass.

Left The sight of snowdrops shows that winter is nearly over.

Right Bullfinch feeding on blackthorn buds.